STREET ART

R. J. Storey

EDGE
FRANKLIN WATTS

LONDON · SYDNEY

To watch some great street art videos, scan the QR codes with your smartphone. See pages 13, 15, 17 and 21.

Franklin Watts
First published in Great Britain in 2017
by The Watts Publishing Group

Series editor: Adrian Cole

Packaged for Franklin Watts by Storeybooks
rita@storeybooks.co.uk
Designer: Rita Storey

Dewey classification: 751.7'3
ISBN: 978 1 4451 1948 9

Printed in China

Franklin Watts
An imprint of Hachette Children's Group
Part of The Watts Publishing Group
Carmelite House, 50 Victoria Embankment
London EC4Y 0DZ

An Hachette UK Company
www.hachette.co.uk
www.franklinwatts.co.uk

FSC
www.fsc.org
MIX
Paper from
responsible sources
FSC® C104740

Photo acknowledgements
1000Words/Shutterstock.com: 10. 501room/Shutterstock.com: 12, 13. AbelTumik/Shutterstock.com: 1, 6. AFP/Getty Images: 22. AlamyCelebrity/Alamy: 16 – 17. CafebeanzCompany/Shutterstock.com: 16. gary718/Shutterstock.com: 6 – 7. GeorgeKoroneos/Shutterstock.com: 21. Getty Images: 5. jonLe-Bon/Shutterstock.com: 8 – 9. iStockphoto 3, 19. jkirsh/Shutterstock.com: 14. looptaggr: 9. OnTheRoad/Alamy: 4. pjhpix/Shutterstock.com: 5. RadoslawLecyk/Shutterstock.com: 18. SamCornwell/Shutterstock.com: 11.

Contents

Street Art

Street art is found on buildings and pavements. Anyone can see street art. It is free.

Street art can be very small. This artist paints on used chewing gum.

Some street paintings are very big. This picture covers the side of a building.

Street Gallery

Street art can appear almost anywhere there is a blank wall. In some towns the streets have become an art gallery.

These painting are on the Berlin Wall. They are part of the largest open-air art gallery in the world.

Street art is only temporary. A street artist does not own the artwork. It can be overpainted or removed.

Stencil Art

Spraying paint through a stencil is a quick way to create a picture on a wall.

Street artists use stencils to repeat a picture or message over and over again.

Banksy

Banksy is a famous street artist. No one knows his real identity.

Banksy

Banksy began as a graffiti artist in Bristol. You can now see his work on the streets of cities all over the world.

Pavement Art

"Great art can be right under your feet."

Some street artists draw or paint directly onto a pavement using chalks or pastels.

Some very clever pavement art tricks passers-by into seeing things that are not real!

This is the same artwork, but seen from a different angle. It looks very different now!

Sculptures

Some cities have sculptures in their parks and public spaces.

he power to question is the basis of all progress. INDIRA GANDHI

In a park in Chicago, USA, there is a fountain that is also a video sculpture.

Art Installations

Some pieces of 3D street art use the surroundings as part of the work.

These pieces are called art installations.

American artist Mark Jenkins is well known for his street art installations made from tape.

" . . . street art. . . creates a visual heartbeat in the city."

Mark Jenkins

Get the Message

IF AT FIRST
YOU DON'T SUCCEED
- CALL AN AIRSTRIKE

Street art is a way of getting a message to a lot of people.

COLUMBUS

Sometimes people use street art to protest about things they do not agree with.

Poster Art

Street poster artists paste the posters they design on walls in public places.

Shepard Fairey

Shepard Fairey is a well-known street poster artist.

He is best known for designing posters with a political message. He designed a famous poster of Barack Obama (see page 20).

The works of street artists such as Shepard Fairey are now just as likely to be seen on the wall of an art gallery as on the street.

Glossary

Art gallery A room, or rooms, where works of art are displayed for people to see them.

Art installations Artwork that uses the space or things around it as part of the work.

Berlin Wall A concrete wall built in 1961 to separate East Berlin from West Berlin. Almost all of the wall was dismantled in 1989.

Fascism A type of government run by an unelected leader who has total power.

Graffiti Illegal drawings or words scratched, sprayed or drawn on a wall or other surface in a public place without permission.

Sculptures Three-dimensional artworks made by carving, casting or shaping materials.

Stencil A piece of paper or card which has letters or other design cut into it. Ink or paint is applied to the surface underneath through the cut-out shapes.

Video sculpture An art installation that uses video projections as part of the work.

To watch some great street art in action, scan the QR codes on these pages or copy the links below into your browser.

13   http://www.youtube.com/watch?v=I5snAOASeIQ

15   http://www.youtube.com/watch?feature=endscreen&NR=1&v=N ziRaGxI8Ow

17   http://www.youtube.com/watch?v=1PnXCqOnYVU

21   http://www.youtube.com/watch?v=iMCxtFmzmxM

Index

Websites

http://www.bristol-street-art.co.uk/
map-of-bristol-street-art
Map of street art in and around Bristol

http://www.bbc.co.uk/news/22664987
Short documentary about Upfest, the
largest Urban Paint Festival in Europe.

http://www.woostercollective.com/
#grid-view
A site showcasing street art in cities around the
world.

Please note: every effort has been made by
the Publishers to ensure that the websites in
this book contain no inappropriate or offensive
material. However, because of the nature of
the Internet, it is impossible to guarantee that
the contents of these sites will not be altered.
We strongly advise that Internet access is
supervised by a responsible adult.